Fundamentals

Games to develop and reinforce mental computation strategies

Orange level

Brian Tickle

James Burnett

ORIGO
EDUCATION

The authors would like to thank the following teachers who field
tested the games and provided valuable feedback and suggestions:
Prescilla Bleney
Gail Fall
Kerry Hoffman
Helen Humphreys
Sharron Johnston
Linda Woodley
Special thanks to Ian Leach for coordinating the field test
and for his many hours spent reading and reacting to our drafts.

Fundamentals
Games to develop and reinforce mental computation strategies

Orange Level

Copyright 2007 ORIGO Education
Authors: James Burnett, Brian Tickle
Project editor: Beth Lewis
Illustrations and design: Brett Cox
Cover design: Brett Cox
Cover concept: Fun ways to reach greater heights with mathematics.

For more information, contact
North America
Tel. 1-888-ORIGO-01 or 1-888-674-4601
Fax 1-888-674-4604
sales@origomath.com
www.origomath.com

Australasia
For more information, email info@origo.com.au
or visit www.origo.com.au for other contact details.

ISBN: 1 876842 83 0

10 9 8 7 6 5 4 3 2

Contents

Introduction

Mathematics pervades all aspects of society and our everyday lives. All business and government services are built on mathematical knowledge. So too are the new technologies that are found in our homes and workplaces. Mathematics is even used in our sports and leisure activities. It is not unreasonable then to suggest that people must know a basic level of mathematics if they are to participate fully in society.

Mathematics curricula around the world are changing to reflect changes in society. Almost every aspect of the curriculum has been reviewed. Computation is one area in particular that has received much attention. There is now greater emphasis on the ability to compute mentally and far less attention given to the formal written algorithm. In addition to changes such as these, there have been calls to increase students' positive attitudes towards mathematics. For example, the National Council of Teachers of Mathematics (2000) has proposed that convincing students that they can do mathematics and helping them enjoy it are important goals for teachers.

Why Mathematical Games?

Games have long been used to motivate students and to help them enjoy mathematics, but there are other reasons for using instructional games in the mathematics classroom.

First, group games foster discussion among students. Using mathematical language is essential for developing reasoning skills and an understanding of concepts. Learning to listen actively to each other, play together and to cooperate are added benefits of increasing social interaction.

Games can also improve students' self-esteem and confidence. The element of chance gives every player the opportunity to be a winner. Therefore, students know they can succeed if they have the skill or the 'luck'.

Finally and most importantly, games can teach. Good games contribute to teaching and learning by providing the materials and ideas in which mathematical concepts and skills can be developed.

Why Mental Computation?

Research shows that the vast majority of calculations used in everyday life are done mentally. In fact, one study revealed that mental strategies accounted for 85 percent of all calculations done by adults in their daily life (Northcote & McIntosh, 1999). If students are to be educated for life after school then they should be encouraged to develop a range of mental strategies for each operation. Mental computation does just that. It encourages students to formulate their own range of strategies and promotes understanding and flexibility in number and operations, known as number sense.

The importance and role of mental computation in mathematics curricula is increasing. Educators now know that students who are encouraged to develop number sense and strategies in line with their own natural way of thinking are far less likely to encounter problems should they forget the written algorithm or when it should be applied.

Finally, mental computation is not the same as mental arithmetic. Mental arithmetic focuses solely on the fast and accurate recall of the answer, and the notion that certain standard things have to be done in order to solve a problem. Mental computation also requires a correct answer, but much attention is given to how that answer is obtained. In short, mental arithmetic focuses on the product whereas mental computation focuses on the product and the 'thinking' process.

About the Series

The six books in the Fundamentals series provide teachers and students with fun and interesting games that build strategies for mental computation. Each game encourages students to develop their own mental strategies. The instructions are simple and the teacher will find it easy to draw out the rich mathematics that is inherent in each game.

The games in the Fundamentals series support the cognitive, social, and affective aspects of learning mathematics. They are designed to

- Develop powerful mental computation strategies.
  Every player is encouraged to progress from inefficient strategies, such as 'counting all' to the more efficient strategies, such as using doubles or making a ten.

- Provide fun, motivating experiences that actively engage students in learning mathematics.
  Every player should enjoy the interactive learning experiences.

- Improve students' problem-solving ability.
  Every player is required to make decisions and select from a range of mental strategies.

- Make the mathematics 'visible'.
  Every player will use manipulatives such as counters, ten-frames, and linking cubes to help them see the mathematics and explain his or her thinking.

- Encourage students to use appropriate mathematical language.
  Every player is encouraged to explore, explain, discuss, and compare mental strategies.

- Increase social interaction.
  Every player can learn from another. They are required to cooperate, to listen to other players, assist them to understand, and share their methods of play.

- Promote self-esteem.
  Every player is given the opportunity to succeed. Through the element of chance, every player can also be a winner.

Game Components

Each game in this book is described over two pages. The left-hand page describes the game itself. It provides the purpose, a list of the required materials, the rules of the game, and a connection to research. The right-hand page details the mathematics of the game. It provides the questions the teacher can use to draw out the mathematics both during and after the game. Most importantly, it also gives examples of student responses to those questions. The right-hand page concludes with several variations and extensions to the game. In fact, with these extra activities, there are in excess of forty games in each book – 240 for the *Fundamentals* series.

Each game in the *Fundamentals* series has the following components:

Purpose

This briefly describes the mathematics in each game. It reveals the operation/s, the strategies that will be addressed, and how the game will develop these ideas.

Materials

Each game requires the reproduction of one or two pages from the book, such as a game board or a set of numeral cards. Other readily available resources may include standard dot or numeral cubes, linking cubes, or counters.

How to Play

Each game includes concise easy-to-follow instructions for how the game is played.

Reading the Research

This reveals relevant connections to research in mathematics education. For example, it may provide evidence to support the teaching of a specific mental strategy, the use of a certain manipulative, or a short rationale for the game itself. The National Research Council (2001a) affirmed, high-quality research should play a central role in any effort to improve mathematics learning. Page 64 of this book provides full bibliographical references to the research.

Before the Game

This suggests ways of introducing the game, ideas for classroom management, or distribution of resources. Sometimes it describes a simple prerequisite activity.

During the Game

Ideas for directing and assisting students are commonly found in this section, together with sample questions and guidance on what to look for in students' responses. Observations and anecdotes made at this stage of the game provide a form of on-the-spot assessment.

After the Game

This component provides the follow-up activities – the ideas for consolidating what has been learned.

Beyond the Game

This section is designed to answer the question, Where to from here? Most games can be varied by changing the rules. Others can be extended by changing the mathematics. This section provides a number of variations and extensions to the game. It also describes additional activities and may make reference to games from other books to help with your planning and programming.

How to Use this Book

The games in this book have been developmentally sequenced. At this level, the focus is on developing mental strategies for all four operations. Use the chart below to choose a game that has a focus you want to develop. Alternatively, you may wish to progress through the book, allowing students time to play each game.

Pages	Game	Key Operation	Focus	Players
8-11	Triple Combo	Addition	Making combinations of ten	2
12-15	Spinning Around	Addition	Making combinations of twenty	2 or 3
16-19	Three Sum	Addition	Adding three single-digit numbers	2
20-23	Double Trouble	Addition	Reinforcing the double-add-one strategy	4
24-27	Roll On	Addition	Maintaining a running total	2
28-31	Take or Tally	Subtraction	Using addition to subtract	1 to 4
32-35	Cat and Mice	Subtraction	Calculating difference	2
36-39	Take Off	Subtraction	Reinforcing subtraction strategies	2
40-43	Headache	Subtraction	Connecting addition and subtraction	3
44-47	Collector Cards	Subtraction	Identifying a difference of ten	2
48-51	Four of a Kind	Multiplication	Using rhythmic and skip counting	2
52-55	First to Forty	Addition/subtraction	Reinforcing the make-a-ten strategy	2
56-59	Double Barrel	Multiplication	Doubling multiples of ten	2
60-63	Criss-Cross	Addition/subtraction	Connecting addition and subtraction	2 or 3

Assessment

Teachers should take the opportunity to listen to their students and observe how they play the games. The 'During the Game' component suggests ways to encourage students to explain and sometimes show their thinking. It also describes what to look for. For example, in a game that involves the addition of two single-digit numbers, identify the students who calculate the total by counting from one. These students should be paired with others who use more efficient strategies, such as counting on or using doubles. In this way, assessment is simply noting how the students think, as opposed to observing if they get it right or wrong.

Triple Combo

Making combinations of ten

Purpose

In this game, students mentally add three one-digit numbers. The aim is to identify combinations that total ten. The students are encouraged to make decisions and predictions based on an understanding of the probability of certain outcomes.

Materials

Each pair of players will need

- A 'Triple Combo' score sheet (page 10) as shown below.

- Three (3) standard number cubes showing numerals or dot patterns 1-6.

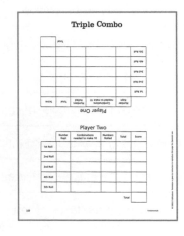

How to Play

The aim is to make combinations of ten.

- The first player rolls the three number cubes.

- If the total of the three cubes is 10, the player records '10' in the 'Score' column on his or her score sheet.

- If the total is not 10, the player selects one cube and records the number in the 'Number Kept' column on his or her score sheet.

- Before rolling the remaining two cubes, the player records the numbers needed to make 10.

- The player rolls the remaining two numbers cubes, records the result and the total achieved.

- If the total is 10, the player records a '10' in the 'Score' column on his or her score sheet.

- If the total is not 10, the player does not score.

- The other player has a turn.

- The player with the greater score after five rounds is the winner.

Example: One player's results after three rounds are shown below.

	Number Kept	Combinations needed to make 10	Numbers Rolled	Total	Score
1st Roll	5	1+4, 2+3	4+3	12	
2nd Roll	4	1+5, 2+4, 3+3	2+3	9	
3rd Roll	3	1+6, 2+5, 3+4	2+5	10	10

Reading the Research

Group games offer a rich context for children's social and mathematical development. Helping children to modify existing games or to invent their own games can extend their learning in both domains (Hildebrandt, 1998).

Before the Game

Have the students suggest three numbers that total 10. Start by choosing a number less than seven and asking students to suggest two other numbers that could be added to make 10. Record these combinations on the board.

Allow two students to demonstrate the game on the overhead projector. Invite other students to suggest which number to keep and which combinations are needed on the remaining two cubes.

During the Game

Try to determine how students are deciding which of their three numbers to keep. After several games, you may want to guide the students to discover that '3' is one of the best numbers to keep because it is possible to roll three different combinations of the remaining seven. (6 + 1, 5 + 2, or 4 + 3.) The greater the number of combinations, the greater the chances of rolling one of those combinations.

If students score 10 on their initial roll, ask them how they figured out the total. If after keeping one cube and rolling the other two, the students still do not score 10, ask them how many more or less their total was than ten.

After the Game

Call upon students to explain their reasons for choosing which number to keep. Six is often a 'good' number in many board games involving number cubes. Do students realize that 6 is not a good number to keep in this game? (Because there are only two possible combinations that total the remaining four: 3 + 1, and 2 + 2.)

Have students work in pairs to investigate all the possible combinations. Observe any strategies they use to ensure that all combinations are found.

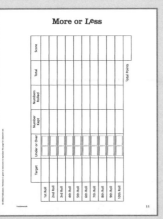

Beyond the Game

- Set a target score, such as 100, rather than a set number of turns to determine the winner. The first player to reach the target is the winner.

- Play the 'More or Less' version of the game using a copy of page 11 (illustrated). This is a game for one player. For each roll (or game), the teacher nominates a target between 7 and 14. Players write the target in the first box and then nominate whether they are aiming for a total that is over or under the target. They then choose a cube to 'keep' and roll the other two cubes. If they are correct in their prediction, they score a point.

Triple Combo

Player One

Number Kept	Combinations needed to make 10	Numbers Rolled	Total	Score
1st Roll				
2nd Roll				
3rd Roll				
4th Roll				
5th Roll				
			Total	

Player Two

	Number Kept	Combinations needed to make 10	Numbers Rolled	Total	Score
1st Roll					
2nd Roll					
3rd Roll					
4th Roll					
5th Roll					
				Total	

More or Less

1st Roll	Target	Under or Over	Number Kept	Numbers Rolled	Total	Score
2nd Roll		☐ ☐				
3rd Roll		☐ ☐				
4th Roll		☐ ☐				
5th Roll		☐ ☐				
6th Roll		☐ ☐				
7th Roll		☐ ☐				
8th Roll		☐ ☐				
9th Roll		☐ ☐				
10th Roll		☐ ☐				
					Total Points	

Spinning Around

Making combinations of twenty

Purpose

Many mental computation strategies are based on a sound knowledge of the combinations that make ten. In this game, students create combinations of twenty. In doing so, the students are required to write two addition facts for each combination.

Materials

Each group of players will need

- A 'Spinning Around' spinner (page 15) as shown below.
- One (1) paper clip.

Each player will need

- A 'Spinning Around' game board (page 14) as shown below.
- A color pencil or crayon.

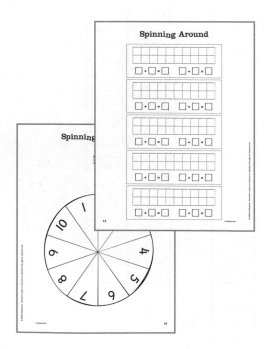

How to Play

The aim is to make different combinations of twenty.

- A spinner is made by following the instructions on page 15.
- The first player spins the spinner and colors the matching number of linking cubes pictured in the first 'twenty' on his or her game board.
- The player then writes two addition sentences to describe the picture.

Example: Jay spins 7 and colors seven linking cubes. He writes 7 + 13 = 20 and 13 + 7 = 20.

- The other player(s) has a turn.
- If a player spins a number that has already been used on his or her game board, he or she misses a turn.
- The first player to create five different combinations of twenty is the winner.

Reading the Research

Evidence suggests that many experiences with a small number of models may be more effective than limited experiences with a variety of models (Hiebert & Wearne, 1996).

Before the Game

Explain the rules of the game and show the students how to use the spinner. Encourage the students to color their trains from left to right and top to bottom, rather than in a random fashion. You may also want to point out that only one number sentence can be written for a combination involving ten.

During the Game

Look for students who have just finished coloring a train. Ask questions such as, *How many more would you need to color to make twenty? How many more (or less) did you color in this train than in your last train? How many more (or less) did you color than your opponent? What numbers can you spin to create a different combination?*

After the Game

Challenge the students to figure out the number of different combinations of twenty that can be generated using the spinner. They should see that there are ten: 1 + 19, 2 + 18, 3 + 17, 4 + 16, 5 + 15, 6 + 14, 7 + 13, 8 + 12, 9 + 11, and 10 + 10. Write the combinations on the board as the students suggest them. Ask the students to rewrite the combinations in a list on their own paper to reveal a number pattern.

Beyond the Game

The students can play the game again without the use of the game board. One version of the game can require them to write two addition number sentences for each spin. Another version can require them to write two addition sentences and two subtraction sentences to complete a fact family. For example, a player could write the following number sentences for the spin shown:

4 + 16 = 20
16 + 4 = 20
20 − 16 = 4
20 − 4 = 16

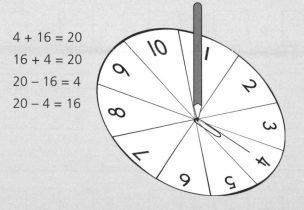

Spinning Around

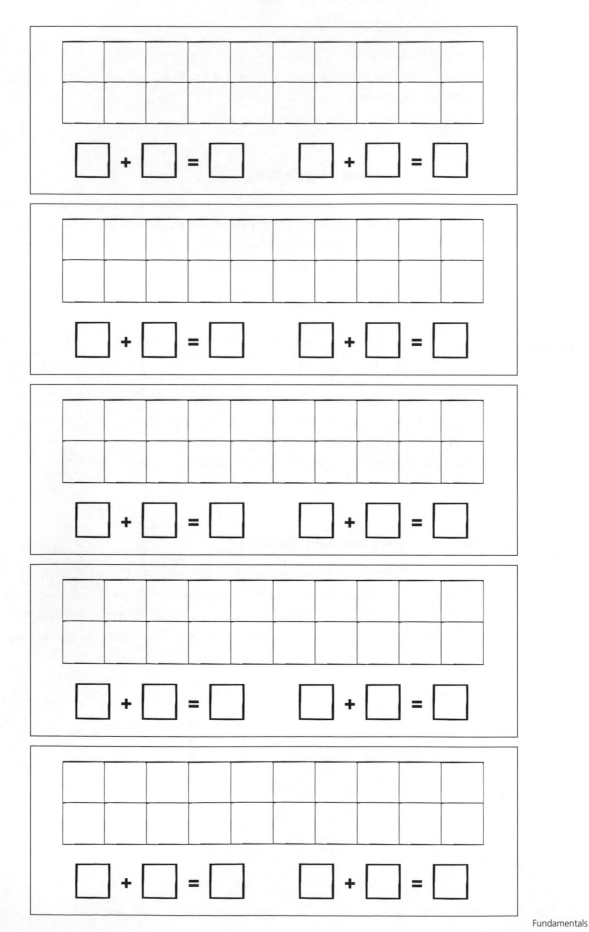

Spinning Around

Straighten one end of a paper clip. Use it with a pencil as shown to make your own spinner.

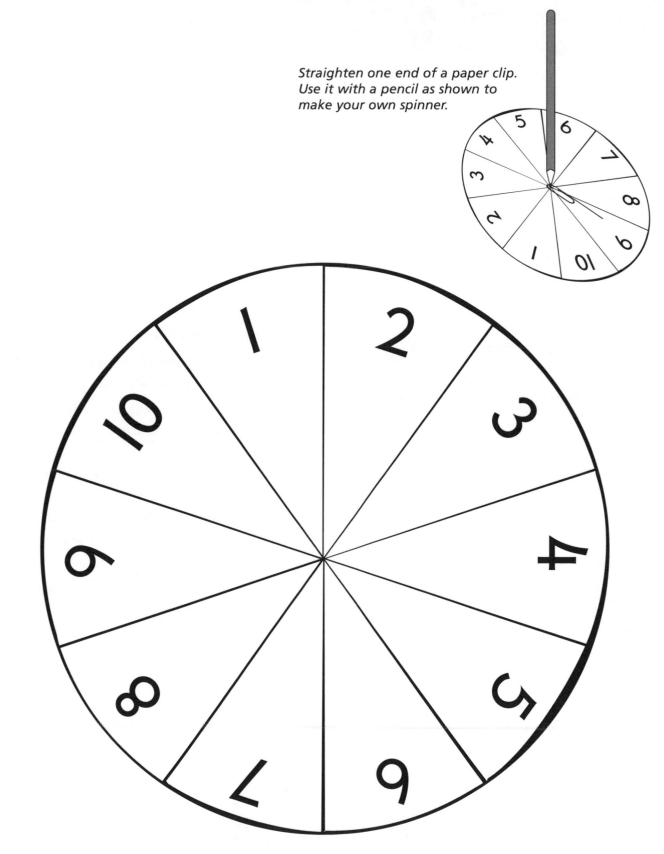

Three Sum

Adding three single-digit numbers

Purpose

This game uses dot arrangements to help students progress from simple count-all strategies to more efficient strategies such as using doubles or making a ten. The students are encouraged to discuss various mental strategies for adding three single-digit numbers.

Materials

Each pair of players will need

- A 'Three Sum' game board (page 18) as shown below.
- Three (3) standard number cubes showing dot patterns 1-6.

Each player will need

- Twelve (12) counters (a different color for each player).

How to Play

The aim is to arrange four counters in a 2 x 2 square or adjacently in a horizontal, vertical, or diagonal line.

- The first player rolls the number cubes and mentally calculates the total of the three numbers.
- The player then claims the answer on the game board by covering it with a counter. If the answer is unavailable, the player misses a turn. A calculator can be used if an answer is disputed. Several numbers appear more than once on the game board so players must decide which moves may be more advantageous for building winning patterns or for blocking opponents.
- The other player has a turn.
- The first player to make a 2 x 2 square or a line of four adjacent counters is the winner.

Reading the Research

The teacher should not be disappointed if a student does not adopt more efficient strategies right away – development may be advancing below the surface at the rate best suited to the student (Isaacs & Carroll, 1999).

Three Sum

5	13	3	10	17
12	7	11	14	9
8	15	12	13	7
11	9	14	8	10
16	18	6	15	4

Before the Game

Introduce the game by inviting two students to play on the overhead projector using transparent counters. Each student could play for one half of the class. Members of each team can offer strategies for calculating the total and suggest where to place the counters on the game board.

During the Game

Identify those students who calculate the total by counting all of the dots or consistently use count-all strategies. Pair these students with others who use more efficient strategies. This will encourage them to explore the possibilities.

When a student needs only one number to form a line or square, stop the game and ask 'open' questions such as, *You need 11 to make a square. How could you get it? Is there another way?*

After the Game

Challenge the students to figure out all the possible totals if one of the cubes is showing the numeral one. Investigations such as this often generate further questions, for example, *Which numbers are rolled the least often? ... most often? What are the possible combinations?*

Make an overhead transparency of page 19. Reveal three number cubes at a time. Encourage the students to share and explain strategies for calculating the total. For example, the first picture may generate a discussion such as this:

Jessica: *I know that 5 + 4 = 9, so I count on 5 more. 9 ...10, 11, 12, 13, 14.*

Jack: *You don't have to do that. There are 2 fives, so that's 10, and 4 more makes 14.*

Jacinta: *Yes, and if there was a dot in the middle of the 4 it would be 3 fives, or fifteen, so the answer must be 14.*

Beyond the Game

* The students can play the game using cubes that show numerals 1-6.

* Have the students make their own number cubes that show the other one-digit numbers, for example, numerals 4-9. They will also need to generate all possible combinations for their number cubes to make a matching game board.

Three Sum

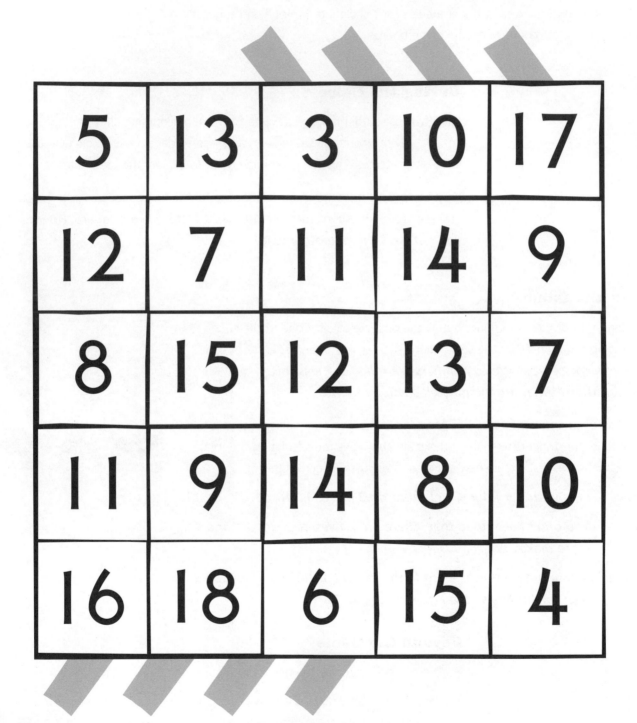

5	13	3	10	17
12	7	11	14	9
8	15	12	13	7
11	9	14	8	10
16	18	6	15	4

Three Sum

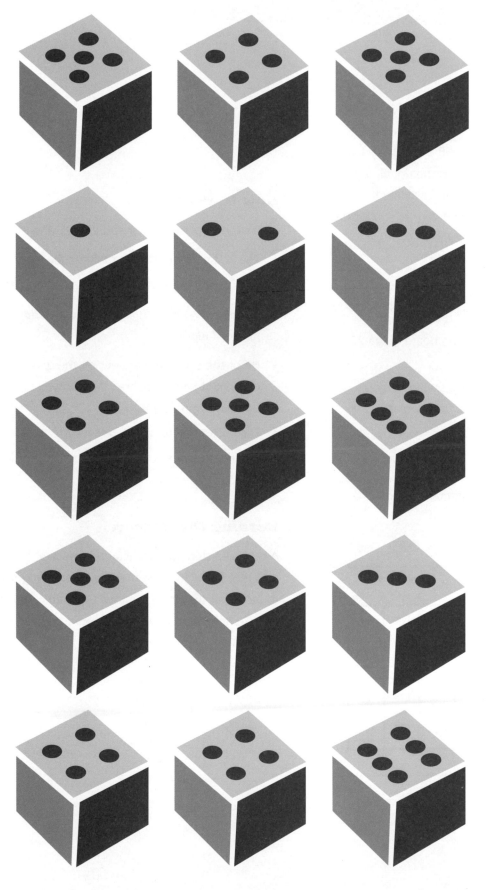

Double Trouble

Reinforcing the double-add-one strategy

Purpose

Using doubles is an efficient mental strategy. This game is an extension of the 'Double Up' game described on pages 56-59 in Book 1 of *Fundamentals* and reinforces the double-add-one strategy. For example, to calculate the answer to 6 + 7 the student can think, *Double 6 is 12 plus one more is 13.*

Materials

Each group of players will need

- A 'Double Trouble' game board (page 22) as shown below.
- One (1) number cube showing numerals 3-8. This can be made from a blank wooden cube.

Each player will need

- Four (4) counters (a different color for each player).

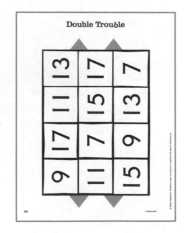

How to Play

The aim is to place all four counters on the game board.

- The first player rolls the number cube.
- The player doubles the number rolled and adds one.

  Example: Wendy rolls 4. She calculates double 4 is 8 plus one more is 9.

- He or she claims the answer on the game board by covering it with a counter. If an answer is unavailable, the player misses a turn.
- Each of the other players has a turn.
- The first player to place four counters on the game board is the winner.

Reading the Research

A powerful strategy for children to possess is using facts that they know to assist them in determining the answers to facts that they do not know. Children can use doubles facts to help them find the answers to related facts (Leutzinger, 1999).

Before the Game

Make a cube train (as shown in Figure A) and hold it up for the class to see. Ask the students to tell you the double that it shows. (4 + 4 = 8.) Add one more cube (as shown in Figure B) and ask the class to tell you the fact they think it shows. (4 + 5 = 9.) Have the students use linking cubes to make trains that shows other 'double-add-one' facts. Select students who have different trains to talk about the numbers they used.

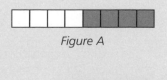
Figure A

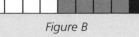
Figure B

During the Game

Point to a number that is not covered on the game board and ask, *What number do you need to roll to get this score? How do you know?* For example, if you point to 15, a student might say, *I know I need to roll a 7 because double 7 plus 1 is 15*. Repeat this line of questioning using other numbers on the board.

After the Game

Invite a volunteer to roll the number cube. Use the number to write a double-add-one fact on the board, for example, if the student rolls 6, write 6 + 7 on the board. Ask, *What is the answer? How do you know?* In the discussion, encourage the students to tell different ways a double might help to figure out the answer. For example, the following two responses may be given:

Jade: *I can double 6 and add 1.*

Jacob: *You could double 7 and take away 1.*

Use the number cube again to write other double-add-one facts on the board. For each fact, have students tell two different ways they could use a double to figure out the answer.

Beyond the Game

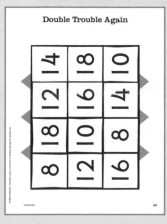

The 'Double Trouble Again' game on page 23 (illustrated) reinforces the double-add-two thinking strategy. For example, 3 + 5 can be solved by thinking double 3 plus 2. For this game, players roll the cube, double the number and add two, before covering the matching total with a counter.

Double Trouble

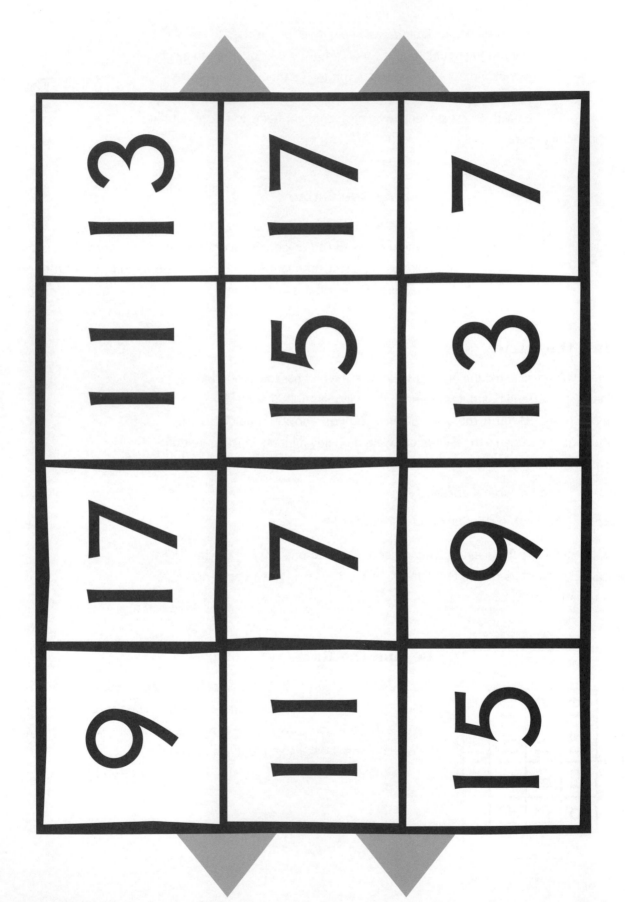

13	17	7
11	15	13
17	7	9
9	11	15

Double Trouble Again

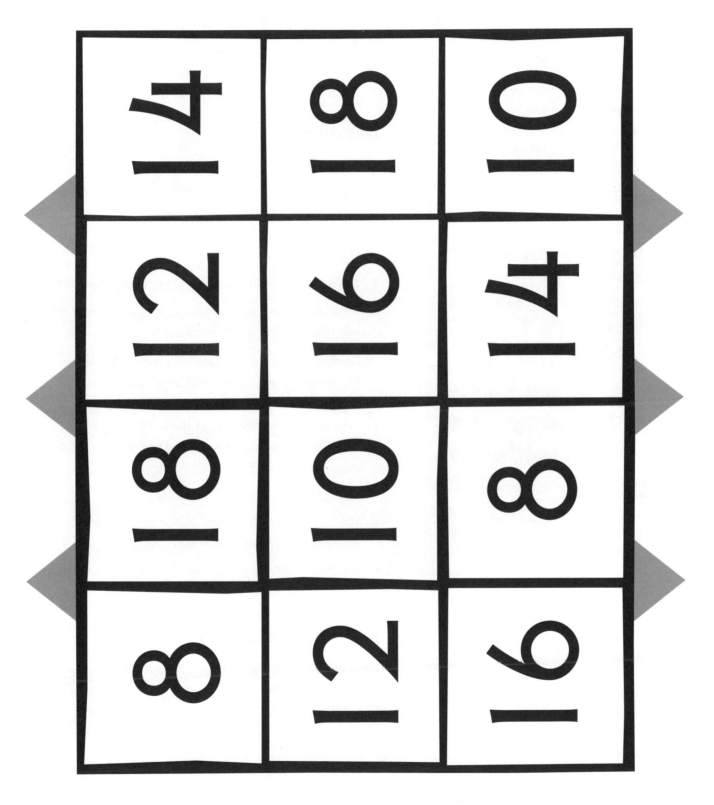

Roll On

Maintaining a running total

Purpose

In this game, students maintain a running total. The strategies they use will greatly depend on the numbers they add, for example, they may count on to calculate 5 + 2, use a doubles strategy to solve 4 + 5, or bridge to ten for 8 + 3.

Materials

Each player will need

- A 'Roll On' score sheet (page 26) as shown below.

- One (1) standard number cube showing numerals or dot patterns 1-6.

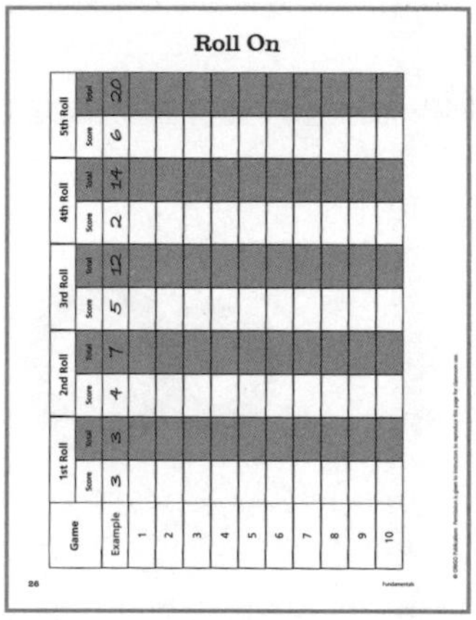

How to Play

The aim is to achieve the greater score.

- The first player rolls the numbers cube and records the result in the first 'Score' column on his or her score sheet.

- The other player has a turn.

- The first player rolls again and records the result.

- The player then figures out his or her progressive total and records it in the 'Total' column.

    Example: The score sheet shows a sample round. The 'Score' columns show that the numbers 3, 4, 5, 2, and 6 were rolled. The 'Total' columns show the cumulative sum after each of these rolls, for example, the result of the second roll was 4 and the total at this stage was 7 (3 + 4).

- Play continues in this way.

- The player with the greater total at the end of each round scores a point. This is indicated with a ✓ .

- The player with the greater number of points after ten rounds is the winner.

Reading the Research

There are different ways that students can be encouraged to move from inefficient to efficient thinking strategies. One technique is to discuss slightly more advanced procedures and why they work (Fuson & Kwon, 1992).

Before the Game

Start by discussing the sample game on the score sheet. Explain the process of finding the cumulative totals. Encourage the students to check their grand totals after each round by simply adding the five numbers in the 'Score' columns.

During the Game

Note the way in which students calculate their cumulative totals. It may be necessary to ask students to explain the strategies they use. Due to the cumulative nature of the task, it is unlikely that many students will be counting all, but some may still be counting on by ones. This strategy is appropriate if the number to count on is small. If they use this strategy for each and every example, you may want to talk about some more efficient strategies. For example, in the sample shown on the score sheet, a student might use a doubles strategy to calculate the second total (3 + 3 = 6, so 3 + 4 = 7) and bridge to ten to solve the third total (7 + 5 is the same as 7 + 3 + 2).

At different stages of the game, ask players to see who is leading (or trailing) and by how much. This will encourage them to calculate and predict which numbers must be rolled for them to overtake their opponent.

After the Game

Ask the winning students to tell how much greater their score was than their opponent's. This will encourage them to use subtraction to compare the totals.

Ask questions such as, *Suppose my score is 7 and I roll a 6. How could I figure out the total?* Some students might suggest a use-doubles strategy and others may suggest bridging to ten.

Beyond the Game

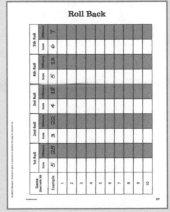

The students could use the score sheet on page 27 (illustrated) to play 'Roll Back'. In this game students start with a total of 30 and subtract the number rolled. The winner is the player with the greater total after five rolls. At a later time, the winner could be the player with the lower total.

During the game, identify the students who use the thinking from their addition strategies to subtract. For example, some students will bridge to ten to add. The same thinking can also be used for subtraction. If a player has 14 and rolls 6, the answer can be calculated by thinking, *14 take 4 is 10. 10 subtract 2 is 8.*

Roll On

Game	1st Roll Score	1st Roll Total	2nd Roll Score	2nd Roll Total	3rd Roll Score	3rd Roll Total	4th Roll Score	4th Roll Total	5th Roll Score	5th Roll Total
Example	3	3	4	7	5	12	2	14	6	20
1										
2										
3										
4										
5										
6										
7										
8										
9										
10										

Roll Back

Game (Start with 30)	1st Roll		2nd Roll		3rd Roll		4th Roll		5th Roll	
	Score	Difference	Score	Difference	Score	Difference	Score	Difference	Score	Difference
Example	5	25	3	22	4	18	5	13	6	7
1										
2										
3										
4										
5										
6										
7										
8										
9										
10										

Take or Tally

Using addition to subtract

Purpose

Using addition is one of the most effective strategies for subtracting mentally. This game reinforces the connection between addition and subtraction. The students are encouraged to use their knowledge of addition to make a true subtraction number sentence.

Materials

Each group of players will need

- Two (2) number cubes made from blank wooden cubes. One cube (Cube A) should show the numerals 1, 2, 3, 1, 2, and 3. The second cube should show numerals 4-9.

Each player will need

- A 'Take or Tally' game board (page 30) as shown below.

Take or Tally

10 - __ = __   10 - __ = __
9 - __ = __   9 - __ = __
8 - __ = __   8 - __ = __
7 - __ = __   7 - __ = __
6 - __ = __   6 - __ = __
5 - __ = __   5 - __ = __

Tally

How to Play

The aim is to complete twelve true number sentences.

- The first player rolls the two number cubes.

- The player then writes the two numbers in one of the number sentences on his or her game board. The completed number sentence must be true.

  Example: Sue rolls 4 and 3. She completes the number sentence 7 – 4 = 3.

- If a true number sentence cannot be made, the player makes a tally in the space provided at the bottom of his or her game board.

- The first player to complete twelve number sentences before making a total of ten tallies is the winner.

Reading the Research

Examining the inverse relationship between addition and subtraction develops adaptive reasoning skills that are essential for algebra (Baroody, 1999).

Before the Game

Make an overhead transparency of the game board. Play a game with the class, inviting volunteers to roll the number cubes for each turn. Encourage the students to add the two numbers to see if the total is in one of the number sentences on the game board.

$$7 - \underline{4} = \underline{3}$$

During the Game

Observe the students as they play. Wait for a player to write two numbers in a number sentence to make it correct as shown (left). Ask, *How did you know to place your numbers in that sentence?* The response will vary, but for this example you want the student to say, *I know 7 take away 4 must be 3 because 4 plus 3 equals 7.*

Identify students who appear to take too long to figure out where to write their numbers. After they roll the number cubes, invite them to share their thinking. Some students may randomly select one of the number sentences and count back one of the numbers in an attempt to 'get' the other number. If so, call upon another student to explain a faster method. The students should see that the total of the two numbers rolled indicates the number sentence to use.

After the Game

Call upon a student to roll the number cubes, calculate the total, and write an addition sentence on the board. The same student can then write two related subtraction sentences as shown (right).

Challenge the students to figure out and write all the possible addition sentences that can be made using the number cubes. For each addition sentence, they should then write two related subtraction sentences.

$6 + 2 = 8$

$8 - 2 = 6$

$8 - 6 = 2$

Beyond the Game

- Change the rules so two players share the one game board. Each player has his or her own column of number sentences to complete. The remaining rules can stay unchanged.

- The students could play the game using different numbers. Give each player a copy of the game board on page 31 (illustrated). Make a new number cube by writing numerals 6-11 on the faces of a blank cube. This cube should be used with Cube A from the original game.

Take or Tally Again

12 - __ = __	12 - __ = __
11 - __ = __	11 - __ = __
10 - __ = __	10 - __ = __
9 - __ = __	9 - __ = __
8 - __ = __	8 - __ = __
7 - __ = __	7 - __ = __

Tally

Take or Tally

10 - __ = __   10 - __ = __

9 - __ = __   9 - __ = __

8 - __ = __   8 - __ = __

7 - __ = __   7 - __ = __

6 - __ = __   6 - __ = __

5 - __ = __   5 - __ = __

Tally

Fundamentals

Take or Tally Again

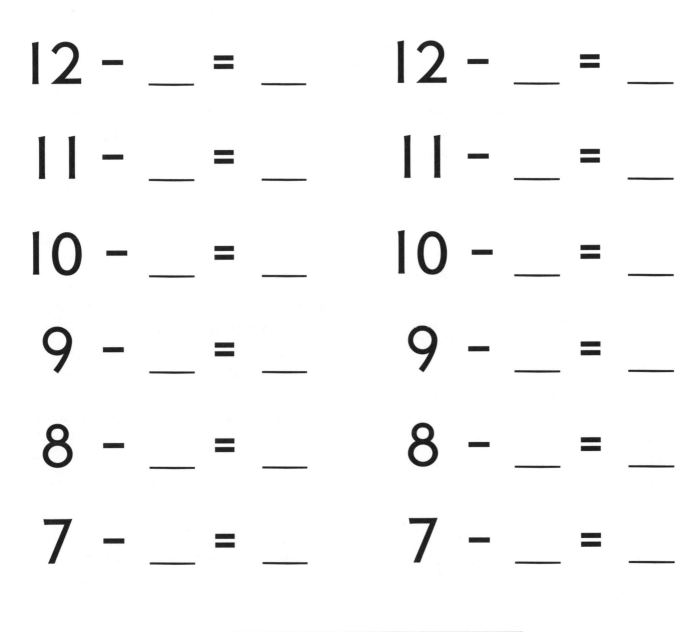

12 − __ = __   12 − __ = __

11 − __ = __   11 − __ = __

10 − __ = __   10 − __ = __

9 − __ = __   9 − __ = __

8 − __ = __   8 − __ = __

7 − __ = __   7 − __ = __

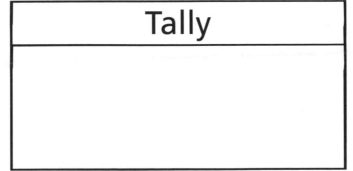

Tally

Cat and Mice

Calculating difference

Purpose

In this game, students find the difference between two numbers. Manipulatives are used to help students see that the difference can be calculated by taking away the part that is the same.

Materials

Each pair of players will need

- A 'Cat and Mice' game board (page 34) as shown below.
- Two (2) number cubes made from blank wooden cubes showing numerals 5-10.
- One (1) counter to represent the cat.
- Three (3) counters (a different color to the cat) to represent the mice.
- Forty-five (45) linking cubes. Connect the cubes to make a train to represent each of the numbers 5-10.

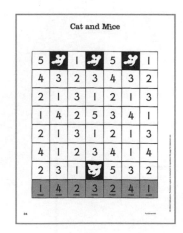

How to Play

The aim is for the cat is to 'capture' the three mice as they try to reach the safety of 'home' at the other end of the board.

- One player elects to play the cat.
- The other player controls the three mice.
- The players place their counters on the appropriate pictures on the game board.
- The player for the mice rolls the number cubes and states the difference between the two numbers.
- The player then selects two trains of linking cubes to match the numbers rolled, places them side-by-side, and states the difference again.
- If the player is correct, he or she can move one of the three mice to an adjoining square that shows that difference. The move can be forward, backward, sideways, or diagonally across. If the player is incorrect or the difference is not in a neighboring position, the player misses a turn.
- There are no positions showing '0', so if a player rolls two numbers the same, he or she misses a turn.
- The player for the cat has a turn.
- If the cat moves to a position occupied by a mouse, that mouse is 'captured' and is removed from the board.
- Play ends when all three mice have been removed or when the last mouse reaches 'home'.
- The player for the cat wins if he or she 'captures' all three mice.
- The player for the mice wins if he or she moves the last mouse 'home' safely.

Reading the Research

Research has shown that manipulatives can help students to correct their own errors (Fuson, 1986).

Before the Game

Demonstrate how to use linking cubes to find the difference between two numbers. Select the trains showing 5 and 8. Place them side-by-side and cover up or remove the parts of both trains that are the same. The difference is the amount that is left over.

During the Game

Invite students to explain their thinking strategy before they use the cubes to check their answers. Do they count up from the smaller number or count down from the greater number? Do they use the same strategy for each and every combination of numbers or do they use an alternative method that is better suited to a particular pair of numbers. For example, given 8 and 6, a student may count down from 8 or count up from 6. However, given 10 and 5, the student may simply know the difference is 5 because double 5 is 10.

Ask a player to point to a square that he or she would like to move to next. Ask, *What roll would you need to make that score? How do you know?*

After the Game

Have the students work in pairs to figure out all the rolls that would give a difference of one. They could repeat the activity to find all the rolls that would give a difference of 2, 3, 4, 5, and zero. The chart (right) summarizes the results.

Ask questions such as, *Which difference do you think would appear most often? Why?* (There are six ways of obtaining a difference of zero – more than any other possible difference.) *Do you think it would be easier or more difficult to roll numbers that had a difference of 2 than 4? Why?* (Easier, because there are twice the number of ways to obtain a difference of 2.)

			Difference			
	0	1	2	3	4	5
Rolls	10, 10	10, 9	10, 8	10, 7	10, 6	10, 5
	9, 9	9, 8	9, 7	9, 6	9, 5	
	8, 8	8, 7	8, 6	8, 5		
	7, 7	7, 6	7, 5			
	6, 6	6, 5				
	5, 5					

Beyond the Game

- The same game board will work for number cubes that show any counting sequence of six numbers. For example, the students may want to make and use the number cubes that show numerals 10-15.

- Two students may want to play 'Cats and Dogs' using the game board on page 35 (illustrated). They will need the two number cubes used to play 'Cat and Mice'. Each player places his or her three counters as indicated. The object is to capture all their opponent's pieces by moving onto the squares that they occupy. Again, the players move by calculating the difference between the two numbers rolled.

Cats and Dogs

5	🐱	4	🐱	4	🐱	5
3	1	2	1	2	1	3
4	2	1	5	1	2	4
3	1	2	4	3	1	2
2	1	3	4	2	1	3
4	2	1	5	1	2	4
3	1	2	1	2	1	3
5	🐕	4	🐕	4	🐕	5

Cat and Mice

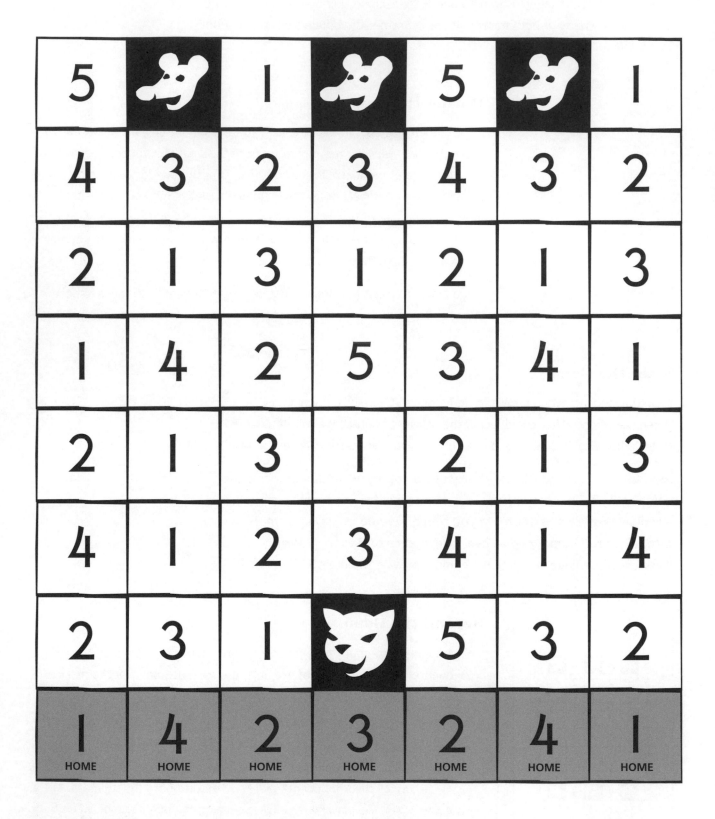

Fundamentals

Cats and Dogs

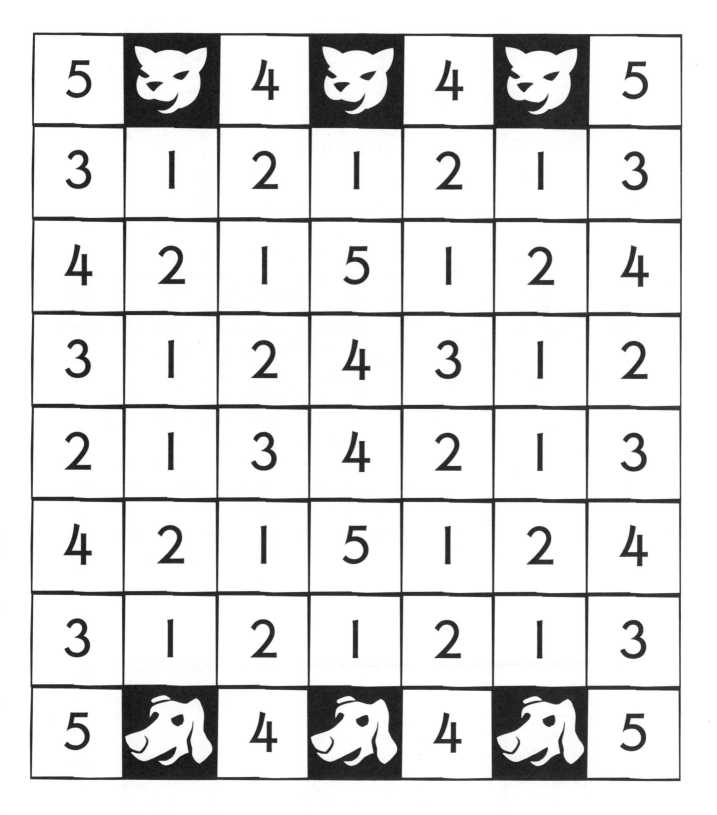

Take Off

Reinforcing subtraction strategies

Purpose

In this game, students subtract 1, 2, 3, 4, 5, or 6 from one- and two-digit numbers less than twenty. The students will need to vary their mental strategy depending on the number being subtracted.

Materials

Each pair of players will need

- A 'Take Off' game board (page 38) as shown below.
- One (1) set of numeral tokens. Copy page 39 as shown below. Cut out and laminate the tokens to make one set.
- One (1) standard number cube showing numerals or dot patterns 1-6.

Each player will need

- Fifteen (15) counters (a different color for each player).

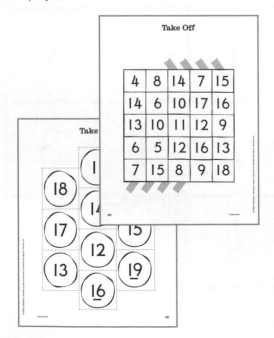

How to Play

The aim is to arrange four counters adjacently in a horizontal, vertical, or diagonal line.

- The numeral tokens are placed face up.
- The first player selects a token, rolls the number cube, and mentally subtracts the number rolled from the number on the token.

Example: Walter selects a token showing the numeral 18. He rolls 4 and mentally calculates 18 − 4 = 14.

- The player claims the answer on the game board by covering it with a counter. Some numbers appear on the game board more than once, so players must decide which moves may be more advantageous for building winning patterns or for blocking an opponent. If an answer is unavailable, the player misses a turn.
- The token is returned.
- The other player has a turn.
- The first player to make a line of four adjacent counters is the winner.

Reading the Research

Sharing alternative strategies with students and encouraging them to share their own strategies will help to expand their thinking repertoire (McIntosh, Reys & Reys, 1997).

Before the Game

Introduce the game by inviting two students to play on the overhead projector using transparent counters. Each student could play for one half of the class. Members of each team can offer strategies for calculating the difference and suggest where to place the counters on the game board.

4	8	14	7	15
14	6	●	○	16
13	●	11	○	9
●	5	12	16	13
7	15	8	○	18

During the Game

Look for opportunities where players need only one more number to make four in a line. Ask, *What token are you going to select? Why?* The student should see that he or she will need a token that is greater than the number that is to be covered on the board. Ask, *What number will you need to roll? How do you know?* Student responses will vary, for example, the illustration here shows that 16 is needed by the player with the orange counters. If a token showing 19 is selected, that player could say, *I know I need to roll 3 because 16 plus 3 is 19.* Alternatively, the player may say, *I know I need to roll 3 because if I count back 3 from 19, I get 16.*

After the Game

Lead a discussion about the methods the students used to subtract. Ask, *Suppose a token showing 14 was selected and 6 was rolled. How would you calculate the answer?* Some students may count back in ones. A more efficient strategy is to break 6 into smaller, more manageable parts. For example, 6 is the same as 4 + 2, so 14 − 4 = 10 and 10 − 2 = 8. Alternatively, the students may use their knowledge of addition facts (14 − 6 = 8 because 8 + 6 = 14). Repeat this discussion for other numbers, for example, ask how they would calculate 16 − 2, 19 − 5 or 12 − 4. After sharing several mental strategies, allow time for the students to play the game again.

11	15	21	14	22
21	13	17	24	23
20	17	18	19	16
13	12	19	23	20
14	22	15	16	25

Beyond the Game

- Vary the game by changing one rule. Rather than returning the token after each turn, keep the token and return them all after the last one has been used. This will limit the players' options.

- The students could play the addition version of the game. Make a new game board as shown. The same rules apply, but this time the students select a token, roll the number cube, and add the two numbers.

Take Off

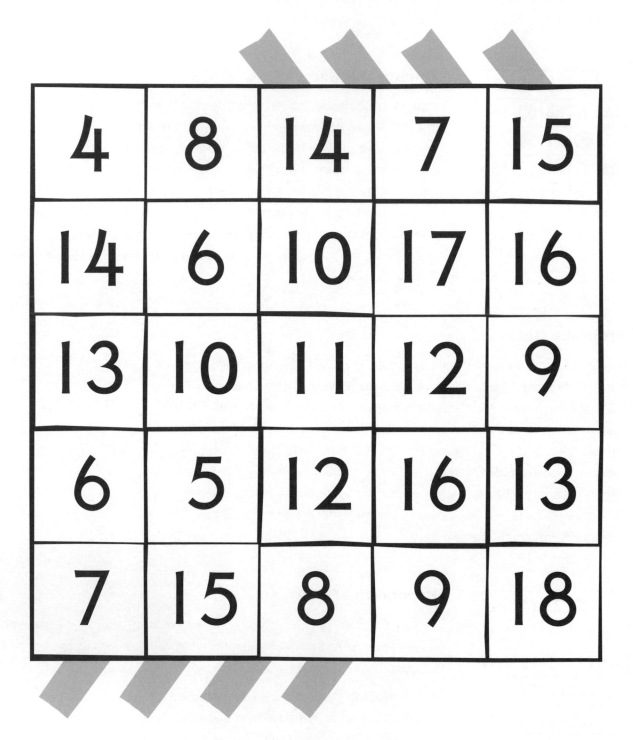

4	8	14	7	15
14	6	10	17	16
13	10	11	12	9
6	5	12	16	13
7	15	8	9	18

Take Off

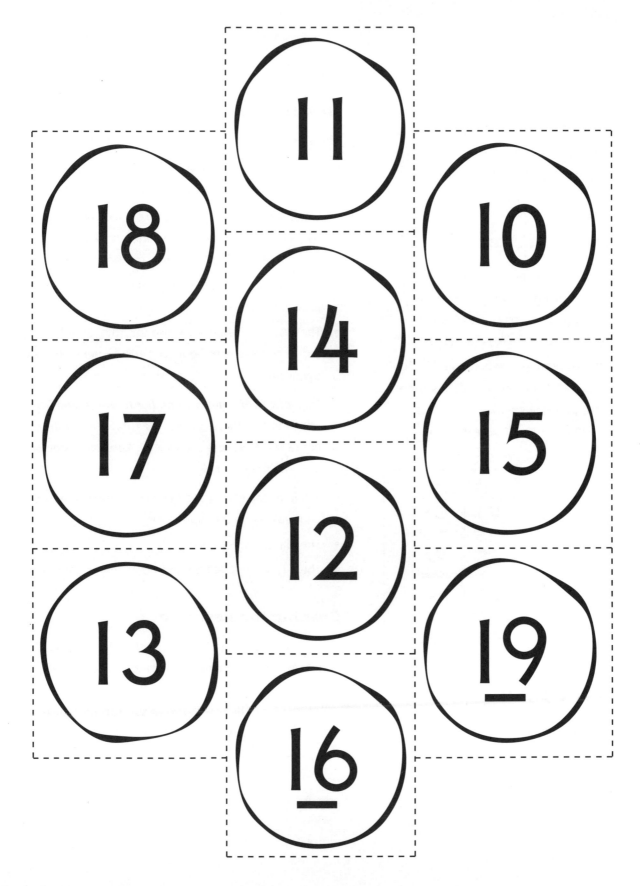

Headache

Connecting addition and subtraction

Purpose

In this game, students are given a total and a part and are required to figure out the part that is missing. Activities such as this help reinforce the connection between addition and subtraction.

Materials

Each group of players will need

- One (1) set of numeral cards for 2-9. Copy page 42 as shown below onto red paper (or another available color). Cut out and laminate the cards to make one set.

- One (1) set of numeral cards for 11-18. Copy page 43 as shown below onto yellow paper (or another available color). Cut out and laminate the cards to make one set.

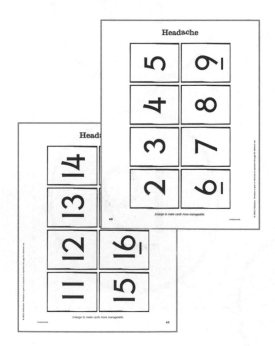

How to Play

The aim is to figure out the part that is missing.

- The two sets of cards are shuffled and placed in separate stacks between the players.

- Simultaneously, one player draws a red card and another player draws a yellow card. Without looking, the players place their card face outwards on their forehead.

- The third player adds the two numerals and says the total aloud.

- The first two players each use this total and the part they can see to figure out the numeral on their own card.

  Example: Elisha shows 15 on her forehead and Kerri shows 9. Marissa tells them the total is 24. Elisha says her card is 5 because 9 + 15 = 24. Kerri calculates 24 – 15 and says her card is 9.

- When all the cards have been used, they are reshuffled, and replaced in separate stacks.

- The players switch roles.

- There is no competition and no winner in this game.

Reading the Research

If students understand the relationship between addition and subtraction, perhaps by thinking of the problem in terms of part-part-whole, then they recognize that counting up can be used to solve subtraction problems (National Research Council, 2001b).

Before the Game

Give the students practice figuring out the part that is unknown. Hold the set of numeral cards in your hand. Invite a student to draw a card and show it to the class. Draw a card, and keeping it hidden from view, add the two numbers, and say the total aloud. Challenge the students to figure out the numeral that is on your card. Elicit a correct response, then encourage the students to share the strategies they used. Repeat the activity three or four times.

During the Game

After a round is completed, ask the players to share how they figured out the missing part. The strategies used could vary greatly depending on the numbers. They will also vary between players. For example, the following responses could be given when one card is 8 and the total is 14 (14 – 8).

Brent: *I started with 8 and counted on 2 to get to 10, then another 4 to 14.*

Bianca: *I knew that 8 plus 6 is 14, so my card was 6.*

Bailey: *Double 7 is 14, so I thought 14 take away 8 must be 6.*

Brook: *I counted back 6 to get to 8, so I knew my card was 6.*

After the Game

Lead a discussion about the different strategies used by the students. Talk about the range of strategies that could be used. Did any students use the same strategy for all the number combinations they encountered? Did the students have a favorite strategy? Were there any examples that the students could not solve?

Beyond the Game

- Combine the two sets of cards and play the same game again.

- Change the rules to identify a winner between two players. At the end of each round, the player who had the smaller (or greater) number can keep the cards. The player who has the greater number of cards at the end of the game wins.

- Extend the game by making cards for numbers beyond twenty.

Headache

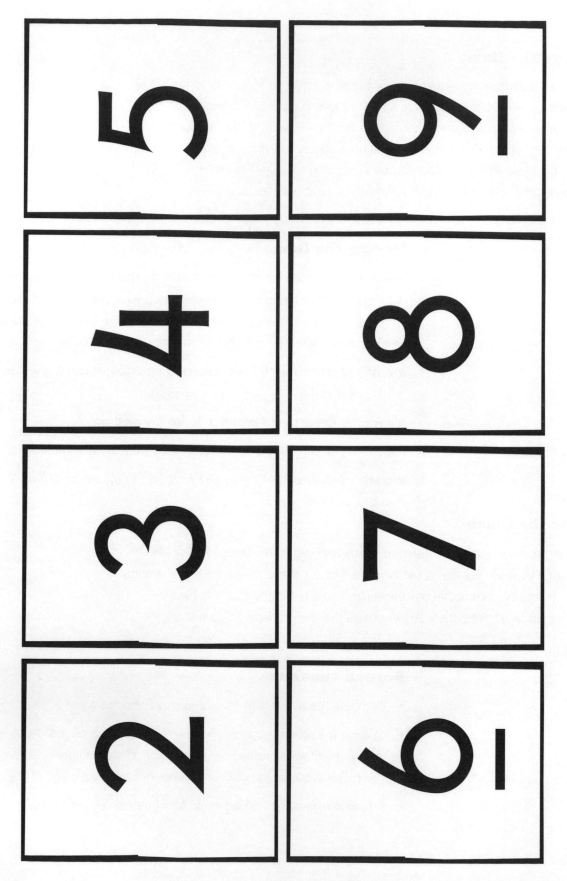

Enlarge to make cards more manageable.

Headache

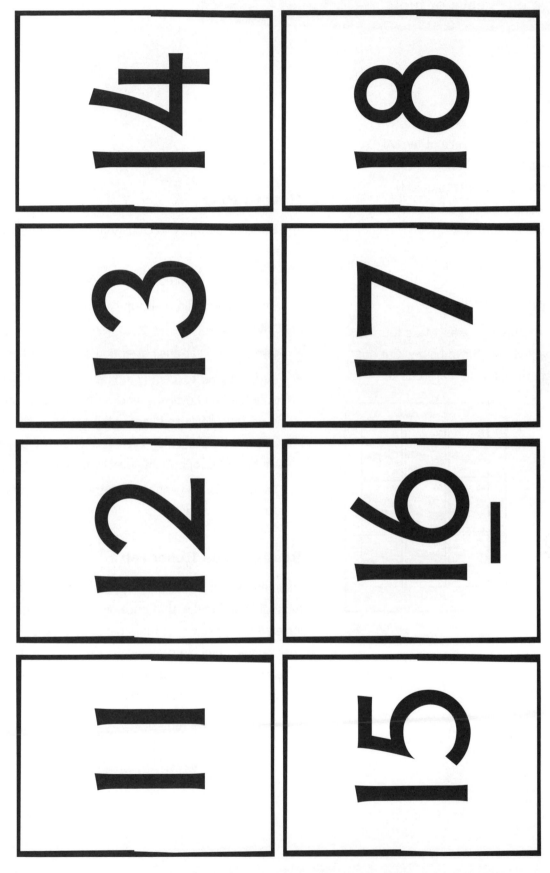

Enlarge to make cards more manageable.

Collector Cards

Identifying a difference of ten

Purpose

In this game, students quickly compare two numerals to identify a difference of ten. All numerals are less than one hundred. The variation requires the students to quickly identify numerals that have a difference of twenty or thirty.

Materials

Each pair of players will need

- One (1) set of numeral cards. Make four copies of page 46 as shown below. Cut out and laminate the cards to make one set.

How to Play

The aim is to identify two cards that have a difference of ten.

- The cards are shuffled and dealt equally to the players.

- In turn, players flip their top card and place it in a center stack.

- Players must keep their attention on the top two cards.

- The first player to identify a difference of ten, places his or her hand over the stack. If the player is correct, he or she collects and keeps all the cards in the stack. If a player 'grabs' when there is a difference other than ten, his or her opponent collects the stack.

- One player is the winner when the other player loses all his or her cards.

Reading the Research

There are numerous parallels between single-digit and multi-digit arithmetic, that once discovered can greatly increase the efficiency of multi-digit mental arithmetic. For example, thinking of 40 + 40 as 4 tens plus 4 tens, increases the chance of a child recognizing the parallel with 4 + 4 = 8 (Baroody, 1998).

Before the Game

Before introducing the game, give the students practice at focusing on two cards. Group the students around a table or on the floor. Pull one card from the four sets and place it face up for all to see. Draw another card and place it beside the first card. If the difference between the two cards is ten, the students should clap their hands once. Continue drawing out more cards at a steady pace. The students should concentrate on identifying a card that is either ten more or ten less than the original card. Repeat the activity using a different card as the point of reference, and then explain the rules of 'Collector Cards'.

During the Game

Stop the game at a point where the two top cards have a difference greater than ten. Ask, *Why aren't these cards a winning combination?* Encourage the players to figure out the difference between the two numbers to support their answer. At a later stage, ask questions such as, *I see 50 is the top card. What number would you like to draw next? Why?* Their responses will vary but they should say, *I would like 40 or 60, because 40 is ten less than 50 and 60 is ten more than 50.*

After the Game

Encourage the students to explain how they know that the difference is greater than, less than, or exactly ten. For example, some students will count in tens very quickly, starting at a nearby multiple of ten. Others will visualize the two numbers on a number line or number track. The position of the numbers helps the students to determine the difference. If it is not raised, you may want to discuss the idea of 'ignoring' the zeros then using their number fact knowledge to determine the difference. For example, the difference between 50 and 40 is 10 because $5 - 4 = 1$.

Collector Cards

Beyond the Game

- The students can play the same game, identifying pairs of cards that have a difference of twenty and at a later time, a difference of thirty.

- Play 'Collector Cards' using four sets of the cards shown on page 47 (illustrated). These cards show the multiples of five between 10 and 50.

- Encourage students to make their own sets of cards. For example, they may want to use multiples of ten beyond one hundred.

Collector Cards

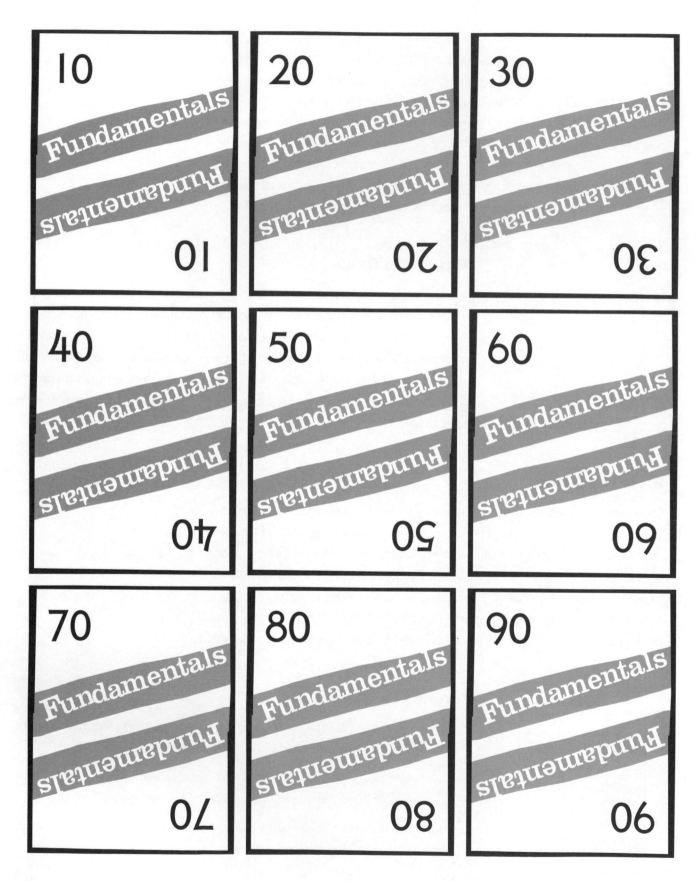

Enlarge to make cards more manageable.

Collector Cards

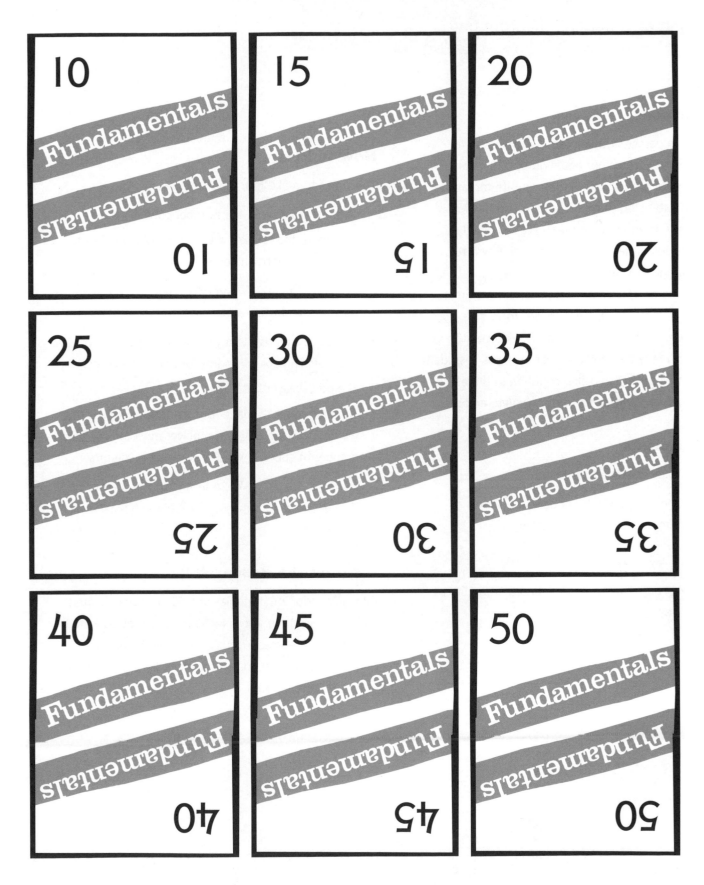

Enlarge to make cards more manageable.

Four of a Kind

Using rhythmic and skip counting

Purpose

In this game, students use manipulatives to construct up to four equal groups. The concept of equal groupings is a pre-requisite for later understanding of multiplication and division. Rhythmic and skip counting are discussed as methods of determining the total. Rhythmic counting involves saying all numbers, but placing greater emphasis on certain multiples, for example, *One, two, three, four, five, six, seven, eight, nine,* and so on. Skip counting is saying only the multiples. For example, a student starting at zero and skip counting in threes would say, *Three, six, nine, twelve,* and so on.

Materials

Each pair of players will need

- One (1) standard number cube showing numerals or dot patterns 1-6.

Each player will need

- A 'Four of a Kind' game board (page 50) as shown below.
- Fifty (50) linking cubes.

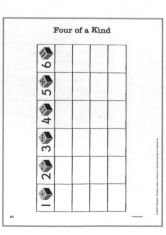

How to Play

The aim is to make four identical towers.

- The first player rolls the number cube.
- The player then makes a tower of linking cubes to match the number rolled.

Example: Troy rolls 4 and makes a matching tower by joining four linking cubes.

- The player stands the tower on one of the spaces in the matching column on his or her game board.
- The other player has a turn.
- The first player to make four identical towers is the winner. To claim a win, the player must say the total number of cubes in his or her winning column.

Example: Russell makes four identical towers of two linking cubes. He says, I win because I have 4 twos. That's 8 in all.

Reading the Research

Class discussion of strategies should be supplemented with activities designed to facilitate more sophisticated strategies. For example, students should be given opportunities to skip count, especially by 2s, 5s and 10s (Isaacs & Carroll, 1999).

Before the Game

Introduce equal groups by asking the students to make five trains of ten from the fifty linking cubes. Demonstrate the rules by asking two students to play the game on the floor or a table while other students watch on.

During the Game

Look for students who have difficulty forming equal groups. Identify those students who are able to see the groups as a composite unit, for example, one group of three is comprised of three ones. These students may be ready to demonstrate skip counting. Encourage the other students to see composite units. Ask, *How many 3s do you have? How many more 3s do you need?*

At various stages, ask students to figure out how many cubes they have in a particular column, for example, *You have 3 fives. How many cubes is that in all?* Observe the method students use to arrive at a solution. Do they know the relevant multiplication fact or do they use rhythmic or skip counting?

After the Game

Encourage students to describe the result of the game. Observe the use of appropriate mathematical language to describe the groups, for example

Mickal: *I won because I made 4 threes. That's 12.*

Mandy: *I nearly won. I had 3 sixes. I only needed one more six to win.*

Ask questions that are designed to encourage students to explain strategies for figuring out the answer. Pay particular attention to the 'fives'. Students are often able to see that 4 x 5 = 20 because 2 x 5 = 10 plus another 10 (2 x 5) makes 20 in all. Find out if they apply this strategy to figure out 4 x 6.

Beyond the Game

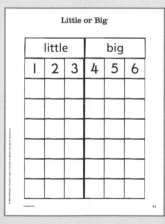

- Two students can use one copy of the game board on page 51 (illustrated) to play 'Little or Big'. Before the game begins, the players decide if they want to play for the 'little' numbers (1, 2, 3) or the 'big' numbers (4, 5, 6). In turn, players roll the number cube. For each number rolled, the player for that number (little or big) makes a matching tower of linking cubes and places it in a matching position on the game board. The first player to make six identical towers is the winner.

- Use the idea for 'Little or Big' to make a similar game board called 'Odd or Even'. The same rules can apply.

Four of a Kind

Little or Big

little			big		
1	2	3	4	5	6

First to Forty

Reinforcing the make-a-ten strategy

Purpose

This game is designed to help students to see ten as one ten as well as ten ones. This realization will encourage students to move beyond count-all strategies to more efficient strategies, such as bridging to ten to solve addition and subtraction problems. For example, a student who bridges to ten to solve 7 + 5 would think 7 + 3 = 10 and 10 + 2 = 12. Although this game involves the addition of one- and two-digit addends, the students will also be using the thinking associated with missing-addend subtraction, for example, *I have 19. How many more do I need to make 40?*

Materials

Each pair of players will need

- One (1) standard number cube showing numerals or dot patterns 1-6.

Each player will need

- A 'First to Forty' game board (page 54) as shown below.
- Forty (40) counters (a different color for each player).

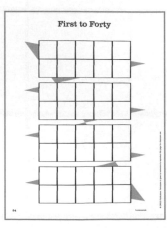

How to Play

The aim is to fill four ten-frames with counters.

- Players must start at the top row and fill from left to right in each ten-frame.
- The first player rolls the number cube.
- The player then places that number of counters in the first ten-frame on his or her game board.
- The other player has a turn.
- The first player to fill all of his or her ten-frames is the winner. It is not necessary to roll an exact number to finish.

Reading the Research

Ten-frames are good for developing part-whole understandings involving the landmark numbers 5 and 10. These understandings are especially useful in addition- and subtraction-fact work (Isaacs & Carroll, 1999; Van de Walle, 2001).

Before the Game

Copy page 55 as shown (right). Cut out and laminate each ten-frame to make a set of flash cards. Flash the first ten-frame for about a second. Ask, *How many dots are in the frame? How many more are needed to make 10? How many more would be needed to make 12 ...13 ...14?* Elicit the correct response and invite the students to explain how they know. Repeat this line of questioning as you show each of the other three ten-frames. Explain the rules of 'First to Forty' using an overhead transparency of the game board.

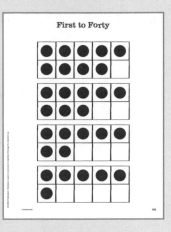

During the Game

Introduce a new rule. Tell the students that at any given time you may ask, *What is your total?* and *How many more do you need to make 40?* The student misses a turn if he or she cannot answer quickly. This gives you the opportunity for on-the-spot observational assessment. Look for students who count each individual square to figure out how many. These students may not yet see ten as a countable unit. Two students who had a total of 21 gave the following responses:

Marcus: *I need 19 more because I need 9 more to make 30 and another 10 to make 40.*

Micala: *I know 20 plus 20 is 40 but I have 21, so I must need 19.*

After the Game

Use an overhead transparency of the game board. Place twenty-seven counters in the top three ten-frames. Ask, *I have 27 counters. What will be my total if I roll 6?* Use counters of a different color to show that one strategy is to partition 6 into 3 + 3. Add 3 counters to 27 to make 30 and add another 3 to make 33.

Encourage students to think beyond 40. Ask, *Suppose I was playing 'First to Sixty'. What would the game board look like?* (Six ten-frames.) *How would you show a total of 46?* (Four full ten-frames and six in the next one.) *How many more would I need to make 60? How do you know?*

Beyond the Game

- Play a subtraction version of the game. Students start by filling the four ten-frames with forty counters. The number they roll must be subtracted from the total. For example, if the first number rolled is 4, four counters must be subtracted from the bottom right of the last ten-frame leaving 3 full ten-frames and 6 (36). The first player to reach zero wins.

- Play the addition or subtraction version of the game using a ten-sided die showing numerals 0-9.

First to Forty

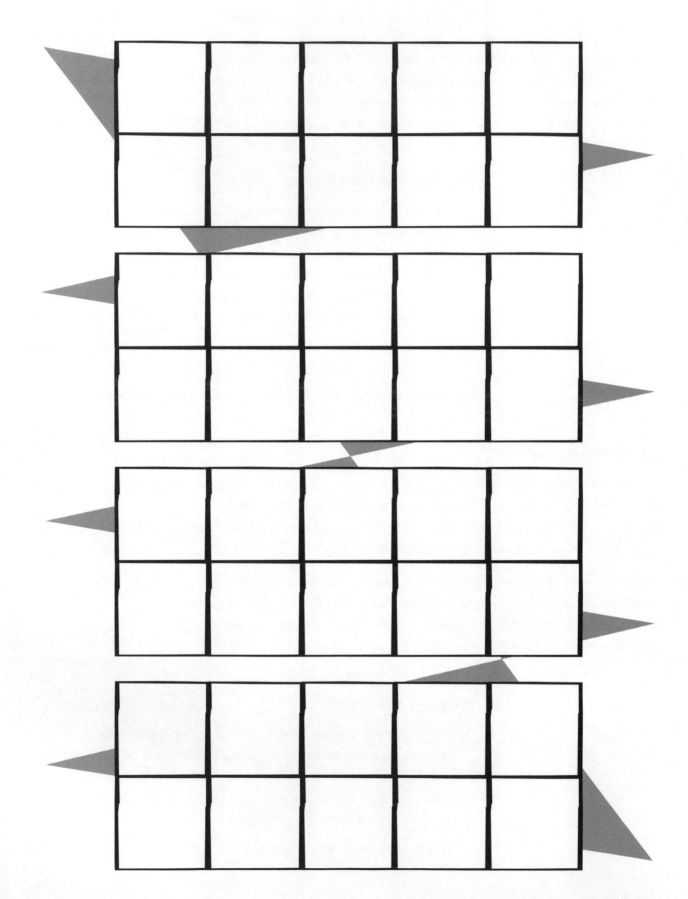

First to Forty

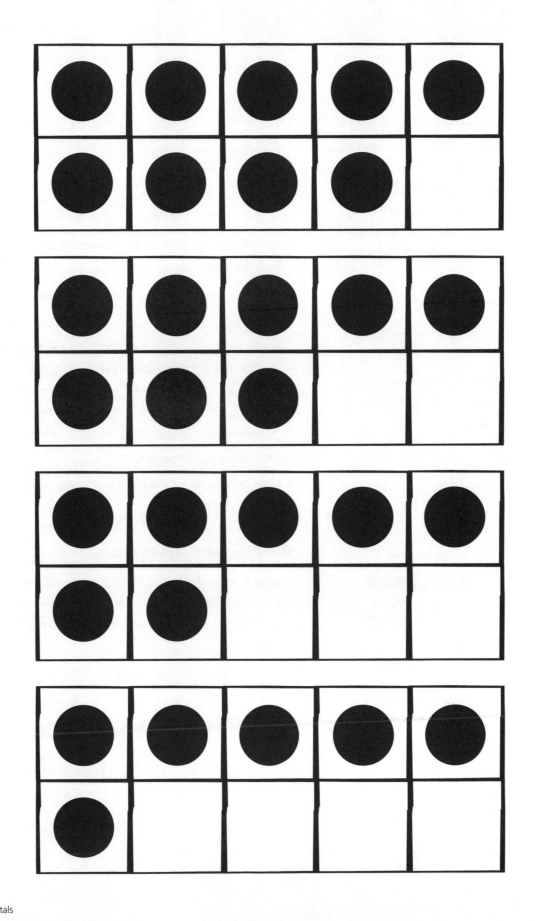

Double Barrel

Doubling multiples of ten

Purpose

Doubling is a powerful mental strategy that is later used to establish the 'twos', 'fours', and 'eights' multiplication number facts. In this game, students double multiples of ten. In discussing possible ways to win the game, they are also required to think about halving.

Materials

Each pair of players will need

- A 'Double Barrel' game board (page 58) as shown below.
- One (1) number cube showing the numerals 10, 20, 30, 30, 40, and 50. This can be made from a blank wooden cube.

Each player will need

- Eight (8) counters (a different color for each player).

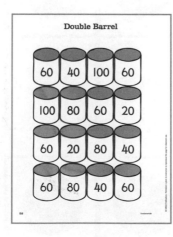

How to Play

The aim is to arrange three counters adjacently in a horizontal, vertical, or diagonal line.

- The first player rolls the number cube and doubles the number rolled.

  Example: Meg rolls 20 and thinks, double 20 is 40.

- The player claims the answer on the game board by covering it with a counter. Some numbers appear on the game board more than once, so players must decide which moves may be more advantageous for building winning patterns or for blocking an opponent. If an answer is unavailable, the player misses a turn.

- The other player has a turn.

- The first player to make a line of three adjacent counters is the winner.

Reading the Research

Games that involve some strategy, some degree of computational skill and the element of chance have been shown to increase students' problem-solving ability (Fluck, 1981).

Before the Game

To introduce the game of 'Double Barrel', divide the class into two teams and demonstrate the rules by playing the game on the overhead projector with transparent counters.

During the Game

Watch for students who have two counters in a line. Ask questions about the number they need to roll to win. For example, if a player needs a score of 80 to complete a line of three, ask, *What number do you need to roll to score 80?* A student may say, *I know I need to roll 40, because half of 80 is 40.* Alternatively, a student may explain, *I know that double 4 is 8, so double 40 must be 80. I need to roll 40.*

After the Game

Use a transparency of the game board on the overhead projector to prompt questions about doubling and halving. For example, draw a straight line through three numbers. Ask, *Suppose I wanted to make a line of three here. What numbers would I need to roll?* Repeat this line of questioning for other three numbers in a line. Wipe away the lines then ask, *Suppose you rolled a 10 ...30 ...50, where must you place a counter?*

If students are ready, translate the results of their 'rolls' into number sentences on the board, for example, *Double 30 is 60, or 2 x 30 = 60.*

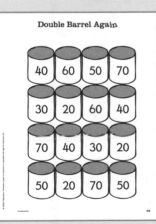

Beyond the Game

- Encourage students to make their own number cube and game board to match. For example, they may want to double multiples that have products beyond one hundred.

- Play 'Double Barrel Again' using the game board on page 59 (illustrated). For this game, the students will also need to make a number cube showing the numerals 10, 15, 20, 25, 30, and 35.

Double Barrel

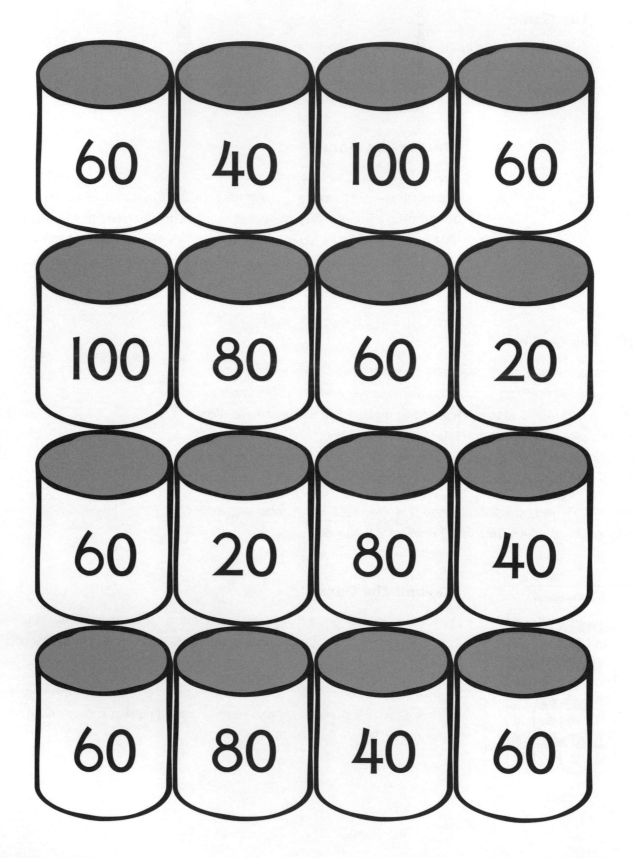

Double Barrel Again

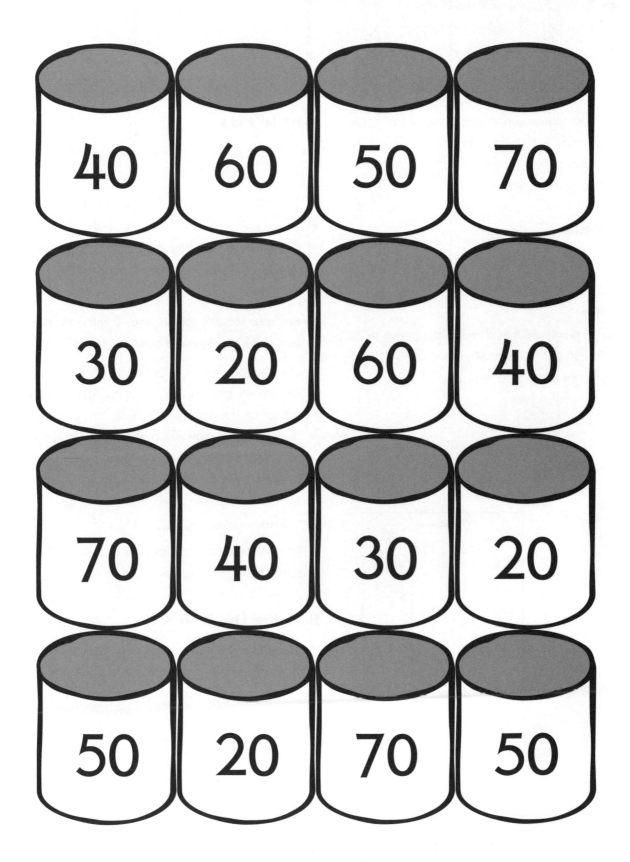

Criss-Cross

Connecting addition and subtraction

Purpose

This game reinforces the connection between addition and subtraction involving two-digit numbers. It requires students to find the sum of two multiples of ten, then cross out two related subtraction number sentences.

Materials

Each group of players will need

- A 'Criss-Cross' game board (page 62) as shown below.
- Two (2) number cubes showing the numerals 10, 20, 30, 30, 40, and 50. These can be made from blank wooden cubes.

Each player will need

- One (1) marker pen (a different color for each player).

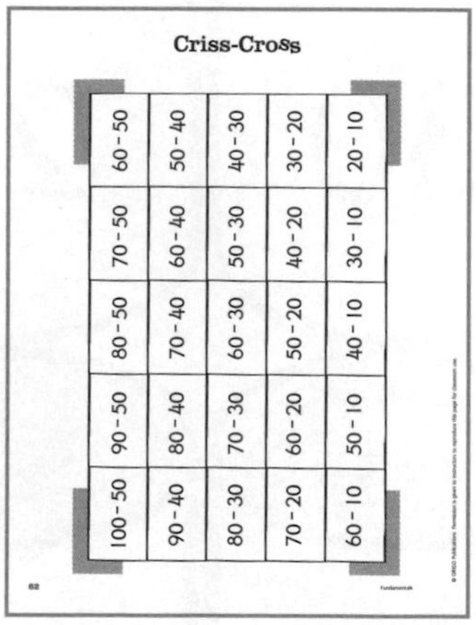

How to Play

The aim is to cross out four subtraction sentences adjacently in a horizontal, vertical, or diagonal line.

- The first player rolls the number cubes.
- The player calculates the sum of the numbers rolled and thinks of two related subtraction sentences. Notice that there is only one option for players who roll a double.

  Example: Melanie rolls 20 and 40 and calculates the sum to be 60. She could cross out 60 – 40 or 60 – 20.

- The player then crosses out one related subtraction number sentence on the game board. Some sentences appear on the game board more than once, so players must decide which moves may be more advantageous for building winning patterns or for blocking an opponent. If both subtraction sentences are unavailable, the player misses a turn.
- The other player has a turn.
- The first player to cross out a line of four adjacent sentences is the winner.

Reading the Research

For students in grades K to 2, learning to see the part-whole relations in addition and subtraction situations is one of their most important accomplishments in arithmetic (National Research Council, 2001b).

Before the Game

Play the game as a class. Use an overhead transparency of the game board to explain the rules then divide the class into two teams. Give different players from each team an opportunity to roll the number cubes and cross out the chosen number sentence. Call upon several of these players to share how they calculated the total mentally.

During the Game

Encourage the students to explain the strategy they use to find the sum of two numbers. The methods may vary depending on the numbers being added. Furthermore, different students will use different strategies. For example, when asked to explain their strategy for calculating the sum of 40 and 30, four students gave the following responses:

Lewis: *I started with 40 and counted on 3 tens.*

Linda: *I just doubled 30 and added another 10.*

Lee: *I just knew that 40 and 40 is 80, so 40 and 30 must be 70.*

Lara: *I knew 4 plus 3 is 7, so 40 plus 30 is 70.*

After the Game

Patterns are the hallmark of mathematics. Have the students study the game board. Ask, *Where do you see the number sentences that show doubles?* (In a diagonal line starting at the top left-hand corner.) *Where do you see the number sentences that have an answer of 50 ...10 ...30?* (In columns.) *Where are the number sentences that start with the same total?* (In diagonal lines from right down to left.) Say, *Run your finger along the diagonal line that starts with 90 – 40 and finishes at 30 – 10. Describe how the answers change.* (They start with 50 and decrease in tens.) Repeat this for other diagonal lines that move down from left to right.

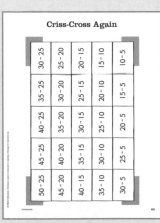

Beyond the Game

- Play 'Criss-Cross Again' using the game board on page 63 (illustrated). For this game, the students will need to make two number cubes showing the numerals 5, 10, 15, 15, 20, and 25. The game rules are the same.

- Encourage students to make their own number cubes and game board to match. For example, they may want to add multiples of ten that have sums beyond one hundred.

Criss-Cross

60 – 50	50 – 40	40 – 30	30 – 20	20 – 10
70 – 50	60 – 40	50 – 30	40 – 20	30 – 10
80 – 50	70 – 40	60 – 30	50 – 20	40 – 10
90 – 50	80 – 40	70 – 30	60 – 20	50 – 10
100 – 50	90 – 40	80 – 30	70 – 20	60 – 10

Criss-Cross Again

30 – 25	35 – 25	40 – 25	45 – 25	50 – 25
25 – 20	30 – 20	35 – 20	40 – 20	45 – 20
20 – 15	25 – 15	30 – 15	35 – 15	40 – 15
15 – 10	20 – 10	25 – 10	30 – 10	35 – 10
10 – 5	15 – 5	20 – 5	25 – 5	30 – 5

References

Baroody, A. J. (1998). *Fostering children's mathematical power: An investigative approach to K-8 mathematics instruction.* Mahwah, NJ: Lawrence Erlbaum Associates.

Baroody, A. J. (1999). Children's relational knowledge of addition and subtraction. *Cognition and Instruction*, 17, 137-175.

Fluck, S. E. (1981). *The effects of playing and analyzing computational-strategy games on the problem solving and computational ability of selected fifth grade students.* Unpublished doctoral dissertation, Philadelphia: Temple University.

Fuson, K. C. (1986). Roles of representation and verbalization in the teaching of multi-digit addition and subtraction. *European Journal of Psychology of Education,* 1, 35-56.

Fuson, K. C. & Kwon, Y. (1992). Korean children's single-digit addition and subtraction: Numbers structured by ten. *Journal for Research in Mathematics Education,* 23, 148-165.

Hiebert, J. & Wearne, D. (1996). Instruction, understanding, and skill in multidigit addition and subtraction. *Cognition and Instruction*, 14, 251-283.

Hildebrandt, C. (1998). Developing mathematical understanding through invented games. *Teaching Children Mathematics,* 5(3), 191-195.

Isaacs, A. C. & Carroll, W. M. (1999). Strategies for basic-facts instruction. *Teaching Children Mathematics,* 5(9), 508-515.

Leutzinger, L. (1999). Developing thinking strategies for addition facts. *Teaching Children Mathematics,* 6(1), 14-18.

McIntosh, A., Reys, R. E. & Reys, B. J. (1997). Mental computation in the middle grades: The importance of thinking strategies. *Mathematics Teaching in the Middle School,* 2(5), 322-327.

National Council of Teachers of Mathematics. (2000). *Principles and standards for school mathematics.* Reston, VA: Author.

National Research Council, (2001a). Looking at mathematics and learning. In J. Kilpatrick, J. Swafford, and B. Findell (Eds.), *Adding it up: Helping children learn mathematics* (pp.15-29). Washington, DC: National Academy Press.

National Research Council, (2001b). Developing proficiency with whole numbers. In J. Kilpatrick, J. Swafford, and B. Findell (Eds.), *Adding it up: Helping children learn mathematics* (pp.181-229). Washington, DC: National Academy Press.

Northcote, M. & McIntosh, A. (1999). What mathematics do adults really do in everyday life? *Australian Primary Mathematics Classroom,* 4(1), 19-26.

Van de Walle, J. (2001). *Elementary school mathematics: Teaching developmentally.* Fourth Edition. White Plains, NY: Longman.